for Ian
in Prince George 1996
Roo Bo

NIGHT WALK

Selected Poems

ROO BORSON

Toronto
Oxford University Press
1994

Oxford University Press
70 Wynford Drive, Don Mills, Ontario M3C 1J9

Oxford New York
Athens Auckland Bangkok Bombay
Calcutta Cape Town Dar es Salaam Delhi
Florence Hong Kong Istanbul Karachi
Kuala Lumpur Madras Madrid Melbourne
Mexico City Nairobi Paris Singapore
Taipei Tokyo Toronto

and associated companies in
Berlin Ibadan

Oxford is a trademark of Oxford University Press

Other books by Roo Borson
Landfall
In The Smoky Light of the Fields
Rain
A Sad Device
The Transparence of November/Snow (co-authored with Kim Maltman)
The Whole Night, Coming Home
Intent, or the Weight of the World

With thanks to those who first published the books from which these
selections were drawn: Fiddlehead Poetry Books, Quadrant Editions,
McClelland & Stewart, Quarry Press. Poems from *The Transparence of
November/Snow* are reprinted by permission of Quarry Press Inc.

Thanks also to Kim Maltman, Andy Patton, Don McKay, Jan Zwicky,
Brian Henderson.

Canadian Cataloguing in Publication Data
Borson, Roo, 1952-
    Night walk: selected poems
ISBN 0-19-541082-3
I. Title.
PS8553.0736A6 1994   C811'.54   C94-931902-3
PR9199.3.B67A6 1994

This book is printed on permanent (acid-free) paper ⊚ .
Printed in Canada

CONTENTS

for Kim

NIGHT WALK

CAMOUFLAGE

The tree which untangles
at the far end of the noisy meadow
stands apart from evening,
does not own itself.

Birds come to it and go
because it is like another
because they are like others.

Free of the sun
which is said to tangle other branches,
it is free of the gossip of likenesses,
and the stars do not sit in it.

The fruit of this tree,
if it has any,
is not seen in the unaided light,
and the eye which sees it
loses need of mirrors,
becomes
the eye-shaped slit
in the mask which an animal
that comes out now to hunt for sustenance
is.

BLUE

As I lay down to sleep
the pines stuck blackly up
like quills in a dog's lip
in the blue chasm of evening
and flowers withdrew
back of themselves like people interrogated.
Like big sad animals caged.

For I lay down in the big city to dream,
but fugitives ran through me.
Mothballs hung among old coats,
teeth collected in the bureau drawers,
trousers twisted on suspenders on the closet door.
Childhood, still confused, comes back imperfectly.
All night long ghosts try on the clothes,
packed close as cigarettes.
They are no one.

ORACLE

The hills would rather float off,
ragged-bottomed clouds,
but the old acacia stakes them to the ground.

On this one of many hills I lie down,
sorting the moments into good and bad.

Today I'm unhappy for no fixed reason.
In the straw hollow against my fingers
a beetle crosses
like a small inlaid box
containing kinship.

ABUNDANCE

The moon: hoof-print in ice.

Someone's shoes chewing an icy path.
The wasted intricacy of each snowflake.
A field without a man in it.
A rusted plow filling with snow.

TALK

The shops, the streets are full of old men
who can't think of a thing to say anymore.
Sometimes, looking at a girl, it
almost occurs to them, but they can't make it out,
they go pawing toward it through the fog.

The young men are still jostling shoulders
as they walk along, tussling at one another with words.
They're excited by talk, they can still see the danger.

The old women, thrifty with words,
haggling for oranges, their mouths
take bites out of the air. They know the value of oranges.
They had to learn everything
on their own.

The young women are the worst off, no one has bothered
to show them things.
You can see their minds on their faces,
they are like little lakes before a storm.
They don't know it's confusion that makes them sad.
It's lucky in a way though, because the young men take
a look of confusion for inscrutability, and this
excites them and makes them want to own
this face they don't understand,
something to be tinkered with at their leisure.

WATERFRONT

The women's bodies lying in the sand are curved like shells.
The men can't take their eyes off them.
The seawater spangles like a drink of champagne,
but the fishermen don't see it that way,
they have their clothes on, they don't care about girls.
They only care about fish. They yell to one another down
    the beach
as if this were their ocean. Meanwhile,
ignorant, the smelts plod into the nets.
Seated on benches, middle-aged women
in magenta travel dresses, going nowhere,
dressed too warmly for the weather,
delve into the sunlight with their eyes closed and pretend
they are dissolving, like a tablet in water.
Only the babies pushed along in carriages
seem to enjoy themselves, twisting their faces
into vast expressions. Their skin
is still translucent. They haven't yet finished
materializing into the world.

OCTOBER ON HURON STREET

Under the bushes the rhythmic gurgling of pigeons,
like a water bag being squeezed
or a monotonous heart
or a man with a limp
jogging.

Every few streets, propped against a tree,
an old mattress. At last unlocking
how many sleepless nights.

How to estimate happiness?
A percentage averaged over a life?

The ideas we carry around in our pockets
are terrible precipices.

This street, this sidewalk
say nothing of the hearts
carried under the arms
like packages tied with string.

But walking along, the body is weighted
a little to the left. It has that
imperceptible limp.

GREY GLOVE

Among branches
a bird lands fluttering,
a soft grey glove
with a heart.

The land at twilight.
Swamp of black mist.
A first planet. A swordtip.
The bird chanting
in a jail of darkness.

This is the last unclassified bird,
the one one never sees,
but hears when alone, walking.

You can see how far I've gone
not to speak of you.
Birds have made a simple bargain
with the land.

The only song I know
is the one I see with my eyes,
the one I'd give up my eyes
in order for you to hear.

OCTOBER, HANSON'S FIELD

Frost chains the pumpkins,
like planets run aground, or
buoys the dead hang onto,
their eyes lit in the loam.

No more flocks of birds
that blow like a woman's gown
from tree to tree.

Hanson's field is empty
except for the sound
of a few last things alive.

I look at the ground
as if it were one-way glass.
The dead can see me.

Past sunset they send up their shadows
to lean against the trees,
like holograms.

FLOWERS

The sunset, a huge flower, wilts on the horizon.
Robbed of perfume, a raw smell
wanders the hills, an embarrassing smell,
of nudity, of awkward hours on earth.
If a big man stands softly, his wide arms
gentled at his sides, women dissolve. It is the access
to easy violence that excites them.

The hills are knobbed with hay,
as if they were full of drawers about to be opened.
What could be inside but darkness?
The ground invisible, the toes feel the way,
bumping against unknown objects
like moths in a jar, like moths
stubbing themselves out on a lamp.

The women sit in their slips,
scattered upstairs through the houses
like silken buds.
They look in the mirror,
they wish they were other than they are.
Into a few of the rooms go a few of the men,
bringing their mushroomy smell.

The other men loll against the outsides of buildings,
looking up at the stars,
inconsequential.

One of them bends down to smell a flower.
There are holes in his face.

MOON

Swathed in a nautilus-curve of cloud,
the full moon seeks out every place.
It smells like ice.
Compared with it the earthly trees reek of patchouli.
The limbs of lovers, their eyes of haunted oil
flicker in the light, the earth a vast hearth.
Such secretive things out there: asteroids hurtle like bricks.
Each creature a clock, ticking out a certain measure of life.
They look at you with their doleful eyes, and you look back.
Tonight the wind isn't wind but a chorus
of transparent masks. You can't see them,
you merely believe. History is beginning to demand
an end to the story. A meteor slides by:
nowhere you have ever been.

NIGHT WALK, THINKING OF ONE WHO COULD
HAVE BEEN A LOVER, NOW MILES AWAY

Down by the railroad. A few cattle
moo to one another in long drawls.
The dark will make statues of them,
just as it turns us stiff and pastes
our eyelids on like little pieces of dough,
taking our will from us,
locking us in for the night.
Someone has found the footprint
of a two-million-year-old man,
but no one ever figures out
where he was headed.
So I walk alongside the railroad tracks,
and under stars loping like long-distance runners
and the blue halo over the field
and the cattle that sleep through it
we do not come near one another.

LIGHT IN THE PINE GROVE

An inland gull with dirty snowy wings
criss-crosses the days. At night
great birds, the houses, nest in fog,
everywhere fog pointing the way, meaning
there is no way. All of us
are so strange with one another
that you and I can barely speak.

All I can do is give little hints
that you won't be able to trust.
That is why the wind at night
strangles the slim daffodils,
bangs on the weakening shingles
and shakes us around.
I saw a little light pulsing in a pine grove.
I saw that I had been growing up
for twenty-five years.

THE HOUR OF WIND

I get into bed but the pillow doesn't turn away,
smooth cheek, it just lies there.
The lilac slaps against the window,
the wind shakes it the way a man sometimes
throws his wife against a wall.
Sweet grapey blossoms,
soon their perfume will fall away
leaving the raw taste of things.
Even the moon gets a rest
once a month in which it dreams
what? Every night I dream the same mess, I know it
the next morning, having to straighten my head.
It is spring again, the poplars have sprouted leaves.
When the wind rushes through them they make a sound
    like angels
beating their wings to announce the end of the world.

THIS IS THE LAST NIGHT

Night drips tar into the grass.
Lamps fall onto the pond, making
accordions of light, but no sound
ever comes of that. Hills
are like the cool brows of dead soldiers;
they don't look back.
Trees are offered up out of the ground, helpless bouquets.
The light of each star comes hurtling,
but the earth never breaks, there's no way
to kill what you most want. All around
the small towns are lighting up or going dead,
whatever they do best, and the frogs begin creaking.
The soft flash of a fish
makes pilgrims of us. It takes so little.
It is the last night, the moon hails on the pond
with no sound, the canoe navigates
through ruins of trees. How am I to tell you
the only thing I know? On the bank
a wild violet opens. A small purple cavern
that no one walks out of.

NOW AND AGAIN

Night should be fuller than this.
Lying on our backs in scratchy twigs,
there aren't enough stars in this place,
the brightest lights are the distant buildings
in a circle around us. Two people
without a thing to say to one another, or things
that can't be said. Right beside us:
whole societies of frogs and insects,
and we in ours.
I don't want to be made of words and feelings.
I don't want to be a body that craves.
We get up and stumble through bushes,
back toward civilization. Who are we
to be holding hands? The pond gives back
the reflections of two creatures a little startled
at being brought up to date
on their own existence.
How old can a person get?
Now and again it seems like it's time
to pass the baton and let somebody else
run their little way into the future.

TEN THOUSAND

It is dusk. The birds sweep low to the lake and then dive
up. The wind picks a few leaves off the ground
and turns them into wheels that roll
a little way and then collapse. There's nothing like branches
planted against the sky to remind you
of the feel of your feet on the earth, the way your hands
sometimes touch each other. All those memories,
you wouldn't want them over again, there's no point.
What's next, you ask yourself.
You ask it ten thousand times.

A SAD DEVICE

A rat, his eyes like glycerine,
like galleries of landscape paintings,
genitals like a small bell, he,
siphon of smells,
mortician gathering in the gauzy corpses,
construes the world.
The grey warehouse of gothic stars,
the gleaming artillery of water,
the flowerbeds like Arabic scrolls,
all of it.

I think my heart is a sad device,
like can-openers.
Sometimes I would rather step between slices
of dark rye and be taken in
by some larger beast.
Men dreaming of billboards,
cars barrelling on and on in a night marooned,
zeroed in on an immense target.

Now I believe the frozen mammoths
in the laundry room
came of their own accord,
not through coercion
by the Sears appliance man.
Not even he
has a cozy life.

Tiny lions in the zookeeper's hair
keep him busily asleep,
but some of us wake too soon,
when our lover is still a dismantled thing
blue with streetlight.

This rat and I
have more in common than most,

having met once.
Now we go to separate nests
and presumably to dawn
with its crossfire of light
meeting in all the other eyes.

COLLECTED LANDSCAPES

Poplar leaves fingering the light.
There is no colour in the body
the colour of the sky tonight.
Now and then
the trunks are naked as my arms
and someone drifts
beneath the thunderheads of leaves.
No one drifts between my arms tonight.

Light wanders down,
a trickle of dust,
to the garden,
blossoms on the grass, discarded.
Easter lilies, unicorns among flowers.
The humans move among them.
One, a horn of carved ivory, leans
on an imperceptibly swelling
tree. I love
the fragile concaves of the body:
the twilight beneath the eyes,
the double hollows
where the ankle once had wings.

Every few years
while you are dreaming
they replace the world.
You wake aged,

are not the same again.
Sunlight deepens the purple ruffled bark.
Shapes startle the fingers,
perfumed fragments twinge the nose,
the musical warp in air warps the ear.
Light is all there is to see.

The sea flakes in the distance.
Under the wind
low to the ground
comes the quiet
of hoofbeats patterings gnawings
of the animals that lived here
and were silenced.
White rafts. Roots mass
below a shifting floral night.

Between the lavender and green arcs
of the jacaranda, when air turns visible
and the throats' strings at last are tuned,
the human voice will play,
one day, to its end.

The stars have fictions of their own.
They come into being,
there may be heroes among them.
In and out of the trance.

Love
is not the only way it is handled.
Loneliness is definite too.
Of most occasions people say
get away with what you can.

There is nothing
of the heart
to get away with.

II

On one's back
flush with earth and open
to the airlessness
of space
the night sky no longer
a meadow of lilies
no longer
a blackboard chalked
with formulae
no longer the city mirrored

the eye finally
lifts the lid
from the box of stars
of one thought
and another.

In the cool channels of grass
water circulates, among the bloodless statues
a summer wind. Blood slants through my hands
as rain over stones.

Your arm over me in the night,
lightning's brief airy buildings flashing
and falling as you sleep and I don't.
These thoughts, the endlessly descending note,
trick of harmonics,
or chemistry.

A soft fringe of sunlight abandoned
on a playing field repeats
in the brain's pink canyons.
So much is repeated,
a rag of light, shred of film held up
again and put away as if

the story will one day be told.
A kind of night
turns in the blue canyons,
a kind of moon pulls over the rim and reflects
the recollected light
on the playing field
seen once
and seen again.
But not again with the eye.

III

White moth,
winged brain
flitting at the glass,
bit of flesh
replete with habits,
what am I to do
with these hands
that will do nothing on their own?
Yellow rose coiled into shadow,
slow fountain,
no one tampers with you.
My arms the colour of dust desiring
another and another,
there are so many reminders of night,
inaccuracies of touch,
messages one contributes silently
to the air.
I lie back and listen
to the sound of thoughts,
like water, like light
filtering over prismatic stones,
no room for the temporary world
which steals over the eye
in the form of
another lover,

another self.
Long enough alone
the senses one by one go dark,
desire a kind of loneliness,
and sleep wanders easily into the veins,
as the inner terrain brightens
with the only artificial light.

IV

There is much one comes to disregard.
As we breathe the slender air between
buildings and civilized trees,
the remaining wildness
is us.
This century no longer a darkness
we're moving into,
but a forest of animals with human eyes,
and you among them,
I among them too.

Minutes are nothing, there is no measurement
of place transforming, chameleon-like.
I need you, need your flesh reminding me
there is no will abstracted from the body.

Shoreline, browline,
all the high places where fragments wash
and coalesce, bringing rocks imprinted with ancient
    creatures,
crystalline, once alive, picked up and tossed away.
By night: a moon of charcoal and ice;
thunderheads,
the mountains' dream of themselves,
crumbling to rain.

THE TRANSPARENCE OF NOVEMBER

The orchestra of the dark tangled field.
The moon holds the first note.

Silver-grey, the old barn leans a little,
just beginning to rise.

Since early autumn the poplars
have been racing one another
and are almost here.

Whatever small flowers
I may have mentioned in summer:
forget them.

UPSET, UNABLE TO SLEEP, I GO FOR A WALK AND STUMBLE UPON SOME GEESE

Bright dime
cut in two, one half
in the sky, the other fallen on the pond,
but no one will bother to pick it up,
the moon will never be whole again.
Up and down the grassy hillocks
they follow one another, walking
in groups under the grey glow.
I haven't even startled them, this is no hour
for a human. Together here they act
differently, like themselves,
warm-blooded, clumsy, bitching
at one another in a common language.
I wish I were asleep. They are large and warm.
I'd like to hold one of them,
hold, be held.

JULY

Blue sky that holds off at a distance,
you can follow the pine trunks all the way up with your eye
to the high branches stilled in sunlight
where birds come and go
from here to the next county.
You can sit forever in an evening
spitting melon seeds,
twisting around the tongue
the few fibers that held
a whole mouthful of sweet water.
It is possible to swallow this
and all of childhood in one gulp,
along with all the wrongs that have not yet happened,
blessing them in advance.
Bright melon sliced open on the table
with all of summer leaking out of it.
Still the children call to one another in the streets
not wanting to come in, but on a night like this
if they stayed out they would learn how to float
like the moon through the pine branches.
On the table the half-eaten melon
is a cave of red meat and black stars,
pale rinds float in the grass,
and the big neighbourhood dog comes to stand
like a hand stuffed into too small a glove.

WILD HORSES

There are horses of sorrow that
never change their expressions,
their faces hang like shadows, as if
suspended from something bright,
bright horses whose shadows
these faces are, horses
that roamed like an ocean wave across the plains
and left them bare, and the sky tells nothing
of where they went, the sky is too bare.

The horses (the dark ones) stand now in a stable,
no one comes to release them,
each face framed in its stall
of beaten wood, wood marred by weather
and the flanks of these horses
that have been here too long, restless,
with nowhere to go.

Now and then riders come to ride them
over the plains, but their expressions do not change,
fixed in the fixed wind, though they are roving
over territory those others owned
when they lived here, they are saddled with riders
and their shadows, they are shadows.

THE WHOLE NIGHT, COMING HOME

Low white garden fences, glossy leaves
of camellia and lemon after rain.
After dinner, walking, just for a breath
of air away from the family.
The Johnstons' yard glistens
though it's not theirs anymore.
Someone else lives there. Still
they're Nick Johnston's lemon trees.

The firs, their shaggy branches full of rain.
The big rock where all the kids used to play,
building forts around it. Now
it's haunted, more than empty.

Through the mist, the clearing rain,
the whole city blinks like a jet on a runway.
You can hear the engines rev, forever, going nowhere.

The bench that used to look out over it,
where we sat for hours, for those few years,
trying out kisses on first lovers: this time
it's gone. Four marks in the ground.
And the eucalyptus trees
still fluttering over it, with stars between the leaves.

We could own anything then,
just by being there when the owners were asleep.
We had the whole city, the whole night.
It's possible to come back
but none of it's yours anymore. It belongs
to someone else. But where are they?
Asleep like their parents? Or have they found
new places, places you don't know how to find
because you don't need them enough anymore.

THE WINDOW

It's so hot you can hear
insects dropping from the trees and the crickets
playing the cracked violins of their bodies in the long grass.
And so the moon creeps up over the hillside
in a surprise attack, running in rivulets
down the sides of buildings, smothering the shadows
in a rash of white violets.
Only the pines have the stamina
to hold their starlike needles inert
as the sparks of meteors cascade through them.
It's so hot that just to lie there
burns the soles of your feet, you walk on a desert of air
lying perfectly still. Thousands of grains of oxygen
sucked in and out of your nostrils as you breathe.
It would be better if there were someone
lying next to you, but you're not old enough for that yet.
And when moonlight soaks the fissures of grass
you imagine the grasshoppers
fucking there.
It's so hot you get up and the floor
crackles with little pockets of air under the linoleum
as you bring the cool washcloth to lay across your feet
and get back into bed. It's not a night for sleeping
but for remembering what it will be like
years from now, remembering this.
It wouldn't seem so hot with someone lying next to you.
It won't ever seem this hot again.

BLACKBERRIES

The eucalyptus shadows hang
like knives, knives that cut nothing,
shadows. A breeze starts up
like a little thrill
going through a crowd. The wet smoke smell.
A shadow shivers over the hills
and the two girls still picking blackberries
down in the bushes stop and listen.
They've been told about this wind. They've been told
it can get you pregnant, that in the dark spaces
between bushes sometimes a man crouches.
That at the sight of a girl a man
just goes crazy, he can't help himself.
They keep picking, but faster. All they want
is some blackberries. Their mothers tell them that someday
they'll get more than they bargained for
staying out this late. They know they should be going.
But the sun leaks out again, dimly,
then floods over the bushes, over their hands and faces,
a heat which turns their skin white again
and sparkles on the leaves. The blackberries
are taut and warm and sweet; the kernels shine
like the thoraxes of solitary ants making their way
across the dirt. The girls have a game
with sunlight, they pretend
it makes them invisible. But around their mouths
and on their fingers the ragged pink stains
will take a long, long time to go away.

MIDSUMMER

Stepping outside, shutting the door. The night air
full of jasmine and the sound of traffic, windy, distant,
people on their own, going places.
Under bare feet the grass is cool, almost damp.
Nothing to do. Only you can't stay inside, in the livingroom
where your family bloats in the undersea light of the TV
or the empty room upstairs which is yours.
Starting up the hill behind the house, the crickets close by
stop suddenly. So you walk in a moving spotlight
of silence.

The hills behind you are a dark wake.
Where you've stopped to sit the crickets
stay stiff, alert near the roots of grass.
On the left a fan of searchlights opens a fake aurora.
Further off the crickets rattle brightly under the straw,
their music marked with sudden breaks
and new beginnings. Maybe you came to see the deer,
the trampled ovals where they've lain—how many of
        them?—together,
but they never come, not while you're near. Tonight,
any night, you don't know why you've come, only
that there's nowhere else to be.
                              Looking down across the bay,
a long arm's reach away the city streams
like a brilliant plasma, a piece of human tissue.
What does this mean? It means
too many things, all tangled together.
The licorice of Queen Anne's lace,
the nothing smell of clean earth,
the sharp resin of raw lumber: someone you've never met
building on the hilltop. Brambles
the deer will feed on when you're finally
asleep in the house again. Raccoons
will drink from the pond in the garden, leaving
dark forked prints in the mud. Everything

will begin again once you've gone inside. Only tonight
maybe you'll stay up here on the hill.
Maybe you just won't bother going in ever again.

THE WAYS WE'RE TAUGHT

So he takes her to a place in the hills where he
thinks she'll give in to him.
That's what he's been taught:
girls can't resist pretty things.
So he shows her how the lights
shine through the trees
and then undoes his pants.
That's what they've been taught,
the girl to let herself be taken
so far and then say no, the boy
to try for anything.
The hills just lie there like rumpled velvet,
and the skull of the moon floats out of them.
This is what it is to be fifteen
and not know what to make of being alive.
The party was loud. If you drink a little
the music takes care of everything,
it lifts you off the floor, dancing forward
at unknown miles an hour until somebody
falls down and has to be dragged outside.
It's easy to drink too much,
to let it all get away with you.
There's always somebody who never learns
what a bottle and a couple of pills can do.
Still, they've always woken up, telling the story
of how beautiful the tall cool trees look
when you're falling backwards.
So nobody's too shaken up,
somebody thinks to put on another record
and keep dancing. Feelings,
they run so much smoother

27

when they're riding on the notes
of somebody else's song.
It's easier to feel anything
once it's been said before.
The girls, they're all looking around
for a boy who'll give them anything,
and the boys know it, they've been taught
to take what they can get.
So he offers her a ride home.
He says he'll show her something along the way.

RAIN

The bay the colour of steel, of a warship
with scattered sun and cloud on its flanks,
the colour of a battlefield
after it's all over,
of a soldier's mind when there's nothing left to kill,
in the immediate vicinity anyway,
and he can rest,
but what is that kind of rest worth?
There's always going to be something left alive.

The water from a tin cup
tastes thin and substanceless,
you can never get enough.
It's not that the first time wakens
a bloodthirst, it's that you cross over
to a country where everything's different,
a country of men
who don't know what they're after.
Everything tastes thin.
You take it all in, trying to get satisfied.
Then you just shut off.

Rain zig-zags down between the hills.
It shatters on rooves, and there are people inside
just sitting around listening.

If you're an ex-soldier you're out walking in the rain,
you're used to it. Hands in pockets,
the sidewalk full of shoes scraping past,
trousers, the bunched hems of dresses under coats.
You look at people from the bottom up.
Sometimes a pair of women's eyes catches
at your throat, at the way it was when you were a kid,
always wanting to know what came next,
like a movie full of possible surprise endings,
which way would it turn out?

But you never expected this. Never thought
the whole thing could just go on and on,
no end in sight, not much happening, just the rain,
the grey sidewalk and the shoes, soggy shoes
filled with other people's lives. The warm women
hurrying beneath their dresses.
Out on the street
you see people in-between things, never
the place they've left or where they're going, only
their faces with that look of expectation.

Except of course for the ones who live out on the street,
who stay there rain or shine, slumped in doorways,
sunk in their own eyes.

Further off the hills are blurred with white mist.
It's coming down hard there too. But from here
it just looks like a white mist that slowly blows and changes.

SPRING

The hills plunge through mist as if their contours
romped, but they're dead-still, made in those shapes
long ago. From early morning
the black and white cows have walked
straight through walls and columns of mist as if
their eyes could only see three feet in front of them anyway.

The hills in the morning: a green so delicate and wild
it almost shimmers backwards out of existence.
The cows stand sideways
on the hill gazing three feet in front of them
into empty air or they move in that slow
stumbling shuffle over the dirt clods. They could walk
straight through outer space not blinking an eye.

The fault opens up five feet wide in some places.
The small earthquake in the middle of the night:
the world swaying so hard it almost falls
out of orbit,
with only the sound of glasses
chattering in the cupboard.

Beside the run-off line: the skeleton
of one of last year's cows.
The other cows just walk around it
as if it weren't there.
Or maybe somewhere in those eyes
like bells too far away to hear
they already know.

At sunset the farmer
comes out of his white house on top of the hill
and watches his cows as if
he wished they belonged to him,

as if their four legs didn't move in their own time.
If they knew a little more
they could just walk off and leave him.

Always the hills and mist are making their mute gestures.
People get the feel of it, that's all they ever get.

The sheep stand around like errant clouds.
The lambs just sit in the grass, brand-new,
they haven't been here long enough to dirty their fur.
They rest awhile, looking around
as if they don't quite know how to behave.
Then they heave up on those scrawny legs
unfolded for the first time in the world.
And right away they get it:
the feel of being alive.
They want to romp
over every corner of those green hills.

IT'S NEVER ENOUGH

Something about the time of afternoon.
Sunlight singes the tall wisps of straw and somehow
nothing's worth doing except lying down and drowsing
in the warm dust, the mint and lemon smell
of eucalyptus. Quick little winds
shiver through the trees and are gone; they hint
at a storm that doesn't come, ever.
And the little earth-tremors that say: someday.

Calico hills. The huge circumference of shadow
around each tiny oak.
You can see perfectly, even at a distance,
the miniature of light and dark in the leaves,
you can see it
with your eyes closed. The dull buzz

of motorcycles cutting up and down the hills.
The buzzing goes round and round
all sunny afternoons like this,
and the interminable construction of houses:
the saws, the hammers clunking away at dead wood.

All the sounds are hollow, and they carry forever.
It's the sound of a crazy person butting his head against a wall.
The sound of a woman tapping fingers to a music
she's making up in her head and isn't telling.

Those bikers. I've seen first hand
how they smash into walls
and come out alive. Finding out
how far they can push those machines,
how much abuse they can take.
They want to see
if their bodies are any different from that,
if a life
is different from that. I know what they're after.

They'll push a woman into a corner where she can't
say no. Even though she knows
exactly what they're doing to her, and knows
they do it just because
they're careless, deliberate.
She's learned to need that violence, that searching,
even if it's secondhand. She needs to know
the world could blow up at a footfall; there's that danger
that makes it all worth something. And she needs them
to come back with that look in their eyes:
that insane sadness that can't be touched.

Something about the time of afternoon,
these bright, empty hills.
A biker shrieking around the short
hard curves like a penned-up goat
cracking his horns on the walls.

But all that is far away, a dull hollow buzz. The sun
sinks low and shows through the poison oak: emeralds and
    blood.
Afternoon's a good time for drowsing,
but evening won't be: the damp darkness in which
if you had a lover you'd take his hand and say:
let's go somewhere warm. But because you're alone
you'll have to remind yourself to get going.
So you close your eyes one more time to feel the sun
going down through the lids. It won't last long. It never does.

STARFISH

Through the rows of glasses a forsaken
streak of light, as on the solitary spoons
the gleaming strokes —
when sisters and brothers meet
in a dark bar at ten in the
morning after many years,
when the initiates of a family come together in the extreme
obscurity of their likenesses,
the closest friends
become bystanders.
The distances we've just come
to be together
would have taken some explorer's lifetime.

Irish coffees at ten in the morning:
cool rind of cream on the lip and the bitter whiskey beneath
whatever we talk about.
Whatever our friends fell in love with in each of us alone
is fraudulent. Whenever we're together it seems
there's an eye loose here, a gesture there, and out of every
    sentence
one syllable we all pronounce the same. As though between us
there is only one
child of our parents, whom we haunt and share.

There are sea anemones that by touch distinguish their own
from the others, and carefully do away
with the others.
There are single cells that choose to live in one
undulating raft
to navigate, synchronously, the waves.

All day we walk among the shops with their identical items.
And stand looking a long time
at what we know by heart.
The Golden Gate in fog.
The Golden Gate in sunshine
the colour of rust, not golden at all.
Of all who jumped or meant to jump,
of all who meant to drown,
most leapt toward the harbour,
the city in their eyes.
Along the dock supports at waterline,
half in half out, the large pink starfish
neither crawling up
nor letting go. Just grasping.
Large pink hands which are nobody's.

BY FLASHLIGHT

Camped out here once, much younger,
with Paul — his muscles all awake beneath the shirt —
whom none of us would touch. Betsy, Jan, and I
lying wide apart in the clearing
like freshly branded cattle,
wet grass at the edges of our eyes.
The icy heat, the paralysis, the wish ...

the stars so far apart up there
you could see between them

but trusted ourselves even less
and so lay there
knowing only what we felt:
those who ministered to "the real world"
were full of empty threats.

The firs jut three feet farther
into the sky-map now.
The flashlight leads us back,
you, my favourite remembered friends: for this we need
one set of legs to share, my eyes, and the flashlight,
grazing frictionless over the ground, as guide.

For my part, I come back
every few years to take a turn through these woods,
our piece of luck for a summer, eight acres
of redwood and huckleberry,
papery skulls embedded in the forest floor, the bulkier bones
we could never assemble: of deer, or stray cattle, or some other
    animal
we never saw alive.
Which of you keeps up the breadbaking, in memory
of that first laughable sunken loaf? Which of you
still moons at fourteen-year-old boys for us all?

Sitting by the fire, muscles tired
from carrying all three of us around.
Funny how little I've learned, when everyone else
has grown taller around me, like the fir trees,
shutting out a little more light.
The taste of coffee, deep at night, when nobody could care.
The bat that sweeps at eye-level through the twilit house.
The hidden inhabitants, the unknown guests.
Huge forests, fostered on neglect.
The sensuous probing spiders.
Lights that get left on all night.
The sudden attack of rain on the roof, anytime.

BAY LAURELS

for Steve Schwartz

The canyons come to me this time
by way of a letter,
folded around bay leaves picked in that place overlooking
the continuous sunlit hills,
the army base at its distance,
and the filmy wandering blue of the bay,
that single noncommital edge.
I've been gone seven years now.
My body must have renewed itself
once in that time, replacing cell by cell so as not to lose
the overall structure.
You've sent the bay leaves as promised, meaning: memory.

The laurels engaged in shadowplay on the ground
where we sat putting things together, as friends can,
who come together so rarely.
All the years of your restlessness.
You belonged to the spirit that was leaving
the country then, leaving
but never for good.
Just one of the ways we've changed places without meaning to.
Even the stamps on our letters: we've begun
to speak with objects, as citizens of places do.
Yours, flat blue and bright
shadowless yellow toward which an unmanned
probe falls, "Understanding the Sun."
Mine, a fleshy romantic rose, focussed
with tiny spheres of dew,
shade-green leaves
spiralling up from blackness. "La Rose Montréal." We've been
apart too long.

More, I notice myself undergoing strange, unkind thoughts.
Perhaps a subtle tampering goes on in the cells after all.

That bare wire in the brain, like touching something cold: *ah yes,*
he's not here, the one you want in certain moments,
when no one else is right.
Those overexposed canyons
of bay laurels where the leaves come from. Until you sent them
I never put together their sweet, smoky smell
with the hills that bore so much walking, it was just
the way those years smelled.

LOYALTIES

Old shoes,
where are you taking me now?
You who've spent a night in the Pacific
farther out than I dared to go —
and I found you again, bedraggled in the morning,
separated from each other by fifty feet of beach,
salt in all your seams, and sand, and seaweed.
That time I thought you were lost for good.
Old shoes, the first my grown feet accepted
without the deep ache that comes
of trying on what others have meant for me. Don't worry,
it's me they're laughing at, those who find us unfashionable.
Our last day upright on the earth
we'll fit each other still.
Don't let them trick you into sorrow.
If they stow you in a box that's too small
in the depths of some unfamiliar closet, remember
the walks we took, the close
companionship of shoes and feet.
Remember the long
mouthwatering days, each place
we rested, just taking it in. We took it in
for a reason, for the time when they'll stow us away
where there is nothing to see, to do, to feel.
And when you've relived it all as much as you need,

when you tire of standing still,
remember the imperceptible holes, how they tore and grew,
the socks, pair by pair, those soft
kittens that came between us, playful, how soon
the walking wore them down.

THE PHOTOGRAPH

for Steve Schwartz

The last carlights are making their way along the edge of
     California hills,
one pair heading one way, another the other,
and the first big planet is beaming
beautiful coded lights at us, variations on a theme
in darkness.
The hills have never been so black.
The car heading toward us enlarges like a dying star
about to vanish and take as much of the world with it.
The other a lava-flow down the hill, fiery red.
Without that small single oak, plateaued by wind, at the edge of
     vision,
the one you planted there with your fine sight,
the one you took care, by accident, to include,
the absolute length of this moment would have fooled us.
I know what the fog protects
down there, between the hills.
Places I've walked, dusty gullies
that floated all manner of things away, in summer.
Places that never existed, apart from us,
though anyone looking
can see the backdrops.
Oakland spread out like an engine, disassembled, in the afternoon
     haze,
San Francisco lit up each night like a control panel,

as if something huge and godlike were about to come in for a
    landing.

The carlights are making their last stab into darkness.
Fog, surf.
Yes. To talk to you is always to touch home.
How like you, to leave that oak, just at the edge.
Your hand in the world.
And every night the same stars keep coming back without
    warning.
Not one of them I can see with my eyes in my lifetime has left.
So. This is a photograph of time in the place we grew up.
Time, which fools us
with moments. Moments that don't exist,
apart from us.

SUMMER'S DRUG

Those nights. They came after days during which my father's
cigarette glowed like a rose caught in sunset on a distant hill-
side. Then he would stub it out and night would fall.

The air would be traversed by strange scents emanating from
night-blooms, and the passion vine broadcast for miles around
its coded message, wound along the trellis. The fruit dangled,
frosted with silver and fur, and inside: a smile of translucent
teeth, a mouth full of smuggled jewels. The honeysuckle thread-
ed everything with white and yellow trumpets, evaporating in a
sweet gas. So sweet that one inhalation inflames the nostrils and
after that is no longer detected.

All night long my parents slept, breathing it, my mother fac-
ing that darkened place she would always roll toward, the open
window to the wild hill. And my father next to her under the
light, fallen asleep in the middle of himself as in a field he'd
been crossing, the book still open beneath his fingers, and the
circling moths, with wings of powdered lead, whirling shadows
around his face.

THE NIGHT-BLOOMING CEREUS

Persuaded by my mother's expertise in the secret and some-
times occult behaviour of the natural world, the night we
were called up to witness the night-blooming Cereus, the
flashlight in my father's hand, its beam leading somewhere
into the ground, while privately my brother whispered:
Cereus is a star.

Older brothers are gifted with natural military minds. A
nimbleness, casual abilities in sleights of hand and eye.
Conducting with suave nonchalance experiments in which
small animals and little sisters serve interchangeably as
prey and pupil, experiments devised not so much from ill-
will as to delineate a testing ground, a sort of school in
which my attendance was mandatory and from which it
was unlikely I would ever graduate.These minor tyrannies
could be counted on to deflect me from the truth of any sit-
uation. Snails. Slugs. A beetle that struck between the
shoulderblades as I ran away.

Every boy carried, in some back pocket of memory, scale
maps of the neighbourhood containing secret and strategic
locations. Tree forts, lean-to's, natural rock caves, even holes
in the ground. That last summer before the forced exile into
adolescence, beneath the acacia tree my brother and his
friend would dig a huge pit, watched constantly by the cats,
their slit pupils evolved perfectly for peering at a distance
through the long grass. Being younger and less able to keep
out of harm's way, I would be ordered to scrape with bare
fingernails all the dirt from the dirt floor of the fort.

Whether the night-blooming Cereus bloomed or grew shy
in the presence of the flashlight, I don't remember.
Gullibility has its dignity. And optimism, eyes. A refusal to
be domineered by mistrust. If my eyes were on the sky at
the wrong moment, praise misdirection, which promises the
longer more adventurous road. It's true enough that stars
are flowers blooming only in darkness. Praise the moment,
if from that moment on I was lost to the rest of them, one
hand still holding a fold of mother's hem, while the shad-

owy cats tightrope-walked along the trellis, mingling with stars and fruit, the slim grenades of the passion vine. Imagination on its tether, I was up there with the cats, who prefer to encircle any event from above, defining its borders like gods.

UNDER THE ACACIA

Under the acacia lit with yellow pollen, beneath the pines where the straw sprays out in a structure of crystals, startled from cool caverns of dirt, the insects laboured, falling over crumbs. In those hours between two and five p.m. it doesn't matter which shady tree you drag your body under, the mind goes walking, slowly, with no relief. Ants, building with crumbs. And sowbugs that play dead in your hand, sequestered, curled into hollow grey balls. Potato bugs climb over the exposed roots, their unwieldy heads burned out and blind. Over the ground the shadows sway, in and out of focus. And afternoon registers, incandescent, along the street of sycamores, whose bark comes free in puzzle-pieces, leaving a raw geography of the world.

Someone must know how the house fits into the street, the street into a map of the world. But nothing that happens inside this house will be recalled, nothing will escape into history. Outside, the night like a developing photograph, moon and stars, the bamboo shaking its paper knives. And how far out of hearing the upstairs windowlight. How far. How grave.

THE GARDEN

Not only the night-blooming Cereus. The intimacy of all living things, especially those that blossom. Any given spare moment we'd hear the chirping of shears, and she'd be out in the garden. Grasping, letting fall. The same precision, the same care with which, the rest of the week, she performed early-morning surgery, routine examinations on pregnant women.

Strange relations, by proxy. Forbidden knowledge we merely overheard but had no right to reply to or repeat. Diseases. Case histories. Half my childhood friends born in my mother's hands.

Her weakness: loud tropical flowers. Their clairvoyance for storm, generating overgrowth: that something might survive. Tent-like shaggy leaves of the banana tree, its rare bursts of fruit splayed out red from the trunk like hands which withered without reaching their true shapes. A dozen kinds of orchids climbed and grew pristine, their flat painted faces enduring the cold rains. Whole continents sprang alive in her garden, ignorant of their origins. The fishpond my father built for her, rock-rimmed, as if a giant had stepped through, leaving a footprint which had immediately filled with waterlilies, papyrus, all the floral props of ancient civilizations. These are the books she'd read in bed, surveying from her high lit window the plot of history, the layered sediment of explicable event. What she relied on to have deposited her safely. Here. Small black print on an illumined page.

One year a single freak frost took from her half the orchids, the banana, the night-blooming Cereus.

A two-year drought and then they were gone: the papyrus, the passion vine, all that remained of her imported world.

Around this time she began to snore, as if to express a satisfaction with sleep, or else a deepening reluctance to return to us. Or perhaps simply to keep my father company in that sound, his sound, which seemed to extend far beyond the room and to explicate his dreams in unknown tongues to the listener.

My father asleep inside a book, my mother among those loud tropicals which blossom. Continents without origin. Diseases without cure. Grasping, letting fall. The withering and the thriving, all at once.

FUSCHIAS

In the evening air: purple bells made of satin, ladies in violet ballgowns. The unopened ones hang like cocoons, slit, a startled magenta creature inside.

From the raw shoots, pale and striated, odors rise up in flames. And the stars freshly awake in the green dusk: crumbs of fire.

There is a terror at happiness, at feeling your own steps, one after another, like minor earthquakes. It's after the uproar of spring, when the sky unrolls those roads into blueness and quiet, that the clouds begin to shuttle through, carrying their cargo.

A paper kite, mauve in the light that has already forgotten us, still tugs at its string, attached to the earth somewhere.

This is when it is first detected, not as a thought, but because of the surprise. When the smell of the earth comes tolling.

THE WATERMELON

Like a cool tub it sat there, in the middle of the night, striped green and silver, hovering on its curved edge. All summer it occupied that spot. When one watermelon was finished, another would be there. Like all things of which there must be unequal portions, it tormented my sister; this was the summer of her turning fourteen. One night, the house asleep, she crept downstairs in her long flounced nightgown and dug the whole heart out. Bite by bite, icy and red beneath the kitchen window.

It's true no one was looking, but I am looking now and in some ways it is still then. Because of the years between us there is a gap, like that between the first up the mountain and the last, though a rope binds them together.

There is a way in which a single act becomes a legend, the way a child's first mispronunciation of a word becomes a family's intimacy, referencing that one instant forever. Morning swelled, gold sparks drifted through the kitchen, settling over everything, the watermelon and its cold oval shadow. The silt of summer.

ST. FRANCIS

For the last few weeks the daylight hours have fallen short and shorter. Transfixed by yellow porchlight to a wicked chartreuse, shadow-plants spring up all around. Enamel primroses, and snowdrops looking down like tiny street-lamps from their tall stems. The garden bears its losses with a quiet we have never accustomed ourselves to: even the crickets have taken their gypsy music elsewhere.

The little St. Francis looks out from his jagged pulpit high on the cedar trunk, clay birds landing on his clay shoulders. He'd be lost without them, for they were born that way, joined. Like all saints he gazes straight ahead at a single point. The black veils of the cedar boughs shade him, for he is frail, and they live here.

As the youngest, I remember when my father and brothers used to work outdoors. They'd go halfway around the house just to douse the crooked ring of cedars under St. Francis with their urine. Standing beside one another or alone they seemed distanced, as if in some animistic prayer.

But I remember St. Francis most for those April dawns when I was the first awake. The amaryllis siphoned its pinkness from underground springs of cologne. The sun would just touch him and he'd blush as if a woman had come too near, and all day the jays would land and take off again, taunting him like delinquent boys, for he was no bigger than they were.

INTERTWINED PORTRAITS

Boidae had all the illustrious markings of her species. Her back zig-zagged with a bolt of brown lightning, she could have slid through the grasses with the lesser snakes, that emblem on her back, and been queen. But she was my father's snake and would blandly curve around his shoulders, push her blunt prehistoric head along his cheek, up through the frames of his glasses, and emerge looking out from his forehead as if he were some strange rock. My father would let her go as she willed, looping about his neck, he with a playful look on his face that hid a private dare he'd made, something he wouldn't share with anyone.

When Boidae was young, only a foot long, he'd coil her up like a length of live wire and stuff her in a pocket along with his stethoscope, to startle the nurses. He delighted in carrying live things around, pretending they just happened to be there. Sometimes he'd pick a fresh wet flower to lay at my mother's place at the table.

But it's not easy to tell if a snake is happy or sad.

Now the cat likes to follow my father around, and my father follows him. They seem always a little lonely for each other.

45

NEAR THE BIRD OF PARADISE

We each leaned, palm down, with all our weight, into the fresh concrete and then it rained, and the handprints in sunken relief turned silver.

Present at this ceremony of hands:

our mother;

our father;

the elder of my two brothers, the faint smile and beard already putting him just beyond reach;

my sister, with the beautiful half-formed breasts;

and next to me my other brother, the one we would each in turn admire;

while the handprints, orderly, grew smaller. Mine the last.

We're born into the family in a kind of sleep, chaotic, unmemorable ... the awakening occurs much later. This archive began not in words, on a day whose details don't matter. Only the handprints remain, confirming as if by chance an earlier existence, beside the bird of paradise inflamed in the twilight, orange and blue.

On awakening though: to be true to that first glimpse! — that was the vow. Never to betray.

And from that moment on I have memories.

THE NARCISSUS

At night the earth takes its place among the planets. The daffodils dim to the ghost of yellow, but their oniony smell seems to colour the stars. Stars of scorched ice higher than cathedral windows. In the streets the dogs move like space-walkers over a dead planet, sniffing, remeasuring everything by smell, dispossessed. In daylight they'd wag their tails up and down the block without a thought. But dogs' ideas are close to the surfaces of their skulls: they sense the strangeness but can't act it out except by sitting at attention in the dim street, their long black shadows sunk into it, the eye of a needle.

A pond on a spring night becomes a musical instrument. Now and then the plucking of the water, where something of its own volition startles, and a cascade of droplets picks out the notes. Just there the pond lies, rimmed with mud, but the narcissus droop their star-shaped heads at the ground, exiled by inches. Exiled and unmirrored.

BEAUTY

On these leaden days of early spring even one stray tentacle of shadowy sun makes the ground steam. There is a slate-green dust which frosts the backsides of certain trees, away from the wind, which three young girls have just discovered. They go from trunk to trunk finding the brighter shades, streaking it above their eyes, posing for one another. A few of last summer's blackberries are left hanging like lanterns in a storm of brambles, too deep for the birds and too high for things that crawl the ground at night. Still the half-fermented juice is good for staining the lips. The girls are just learning about beauty.

One day they'll be shown what their own beauty or lack of it will do to them. Not one day, but many nights, nights they'll lie alone sifting through incidents, certain instances which are the only analogue of those steeply lengthening bones, the breasts filling calmly, immutably as lakes taking in all that stormy and random rain.

CALLA LILIES

Quivering manzanita, alive with silver rain, a tree of ball bearings! They go scattering, bouncing, as the birds lunge and recover and fences cross, recross the county, stilled woodgrain whorling like spring creeks. Back of the house, over the septic tank, on high crisp stems the lilies have risen, a whole monastery of them, cowls faintly aglow in the tree-shade. The clouds, the little ones, won't say where they're going, just that they're playing up there, they'll never tire. Spring: so casual. A clump of ferns sticking up like the necks of buried violins. As if we were the ones who were off else-where, all those lost months, degraded by sorrow, in self-made darkness and rain.

BEFORE THE FIRST BIRD THINKS TO BEAR ITS WEIGHT FROM THE BRANCH

Each day before dawn comes a false dawn. It fools even the birds. They come flying, still asleep, to take up their places along the phone lines and relieve them of that unresolved talk. Such chaotic chirping! And then, sleep-flying back to their branches, falling silent for another four hours.

Cobwebs caught in the bushes: grandiose ruins of an obscure architecture. Meadow mists, siphoned and beckoned out of earth and air, blown and meandered. A lone spider, severed hand of winter, stringing up yet another grand, withering snowflake. But the thing I meant to show you, what this little walk through the woods is for: see it, under that bush. Still lying there, new to death, giving off a faint negative charge. Look how the wind flickers its fur in a par-ody of running. How wind enters its mouth, but not as breath. And the eyes, gelled in a line of sight snapped side-ways, invisible as the beam of a flashlight left on at dawn.

The wind keeps coming from different sides as if, not the wind, but the directions themselves were changing. I needed to show you this. Maybe you'll explain what it means to tell us, lying there like that, after whatever took place in the dark. Lying on the loosely braided needles, the little silver roses fallen from the pines. In the off-light before sunrise, before the first bird thinks to bear its weight from the branch.

THE RIVER

One day we went wading up the river, my aunt, my mother, and I. Stripped to our underclothes, our bottoms like balloons floating along the surface, the river wide and dusty, a green glass whose edges riffled among debris and weeds. Most of an afternoon we spent wading away from our clothes, while the water gave without a brain, caressing and inanimate, and our feet never quite touched ground, billowing along in soft river silt.

The sky of that day does not fade, blue and matter-of-fact as any day in summer, with the high migration of clouds, as always, restless for the ocean. When at last the sun squinting through the underbrush began to divide each rock from its shadow, we too could see that our own shadows had come for us. We turned around and made our way out of the river then, dripping, back to the bank where we began.

As we dressed I grew awkward, tripping over nothing. Already the crickets and the frogs had begun their nightly lessons, practising out loud, and painlessly. That day my mother and aunt had been as sisters again, while I trailed along behind, more of a ghost, or a wandering bit of my father, so that pulling on the cold clothes again was like tugging twelve times, twelve times on the bell-rope which signals the end of one more day of happiness.

A SENSE OF PROPORTION

It is said the garden dreams during the day. When the light is brightest, green things turn inward, they sleep. And it must be true. For all during the dark, the wind couriers between trees. First one rustles, then another. Messages are borne many hundreds of miles in this way unimpeded.

Whether pine is understood by the cypress isn't known. Or oak by cedar, elm by sycamore. Yet bark may dilate or buds seize up in accordance with auguries concerning insects or weather. Each tree prepares itself by waking the others.

The branches hold ultra-still until we've passed safely under them, for ineptitude is dangerous, though sometimes, from excitement, they quiver. But not because of us! They are intercepting knowledge. That sweet heady smell is no smell at all. And imagine us thinking we have the nose for it.

CLOSED UNIVERSE

A fine perspiration falls from the trees at the height of summer after weeks of no rain. If you sit near them with the wind blowing your way, every few seconds you'll be pinpricked with dew. Tonight, a Thursday night, there is a comet scheduled to pass close to the world, showering down meteors. And everyone, with upended faces, is reminded of Gilles Villeneuve, the race car driver thrown from his car, who, in these few airborne moments, is replaced with even faster, riskier thoughts.

If you sit still long enough, through an entire summer, eventually the fine flowers of the eugenia will somersault, daubed with pollen, into your coffee or your wine, depending upon the hour of day. And the human clockwork, then, tending toward a fateful accuracy, will force you to rise and go indoors, to reappear only when it is once again time to strike the pose and the hour.

SISTERS

Fathoms down through the trees, those men who appear on
fall mornings to build and rebuild the world of streets and
houses, those strangers in workgloves: if they had looked
up, how easily they could have seen. My sister standing on
the fallen nightgown letting the sun touch her breasts
through the window. Wanting to be seen — or just to be
warm. It was the year our difference in age set us in exact
proportion to each other.

The soft blur of notes near middle C, the swaying afternoon
full of bees that lived in her throat as she read me stories.
Saturday nights when she'd let me dress her, a huge beautiful
doll twice my size. She and her best friend in the bathroom
light as they made themselves up: their mirrored eyes like the
dishes of telescopes at a great distance. Able to see on a grand
scale, oblique and accurate.

And I sat around in the desert light of that house at night,
and fell asleep waiting. All the fall clocks set back to regain
one lost hour. In a polka-dot dress she'd go, into the autumn
night full of stars, fathoms down through the trees, to the
world of streets and strangers. Random carhorns, then, in the
distance. A distance at which anger sounds like longing.

NIGHT SNAILS

Imperturbably sideways, they slide, barely grazing the
rough retaining wall which, now and then, holds back a
stray daffodil. Adhering against all gravity, gracious and
slow as a chess game in which the pieces only seem to move
at random, horned shadows glide in and out of checkmate,
where the daffodils cast themselves huge under enchanted
lamps. Pruned flat against the house and pinned there, the
pear bears freckled fruit whose flesh is white, unworldly,
grained like the tongue itself, and may be eaten as a tonic
against loneliness.

FOLKLORE

They come at dusk down the hill to the apple trees, a few deer. They come out before stars to rub against the bark, scarring the fruit. But what deer really love to eat are roses. The moss rose they'll eat to the ground.

If you've never seen deer near the city, they move as they chew, feeding on apples, like women used to high heels and lipstick. Then they venture closer. If you love your roses you'll enclose them in cages of wire as you would a song-bird.

There is the fruitless beauty of the household, and then there is the beauty of the field. Their high cheekbones as they feed on the last roses.

And that which now comes alight, the house you grew up in: sometimes it is a lantern small enough to carry before you in one hand.

WHERE THERE IS DARKNESS

Out on the front porch, late, the earth still emanating collective warmth. If, on a summer night, to come back is to let the vision blur, then it is not an eye for an eye, at least, but one eye superimposing upon the other the past, ghosted.

And so to come back at that slight disadvantage, not so much amnesiac, but as from long disuse, finding one has lost, almost, the ability. The need to pretend not to recognize. So much complicity.

A disused basketball hoop at midnight, kids long grown up and gone, all residential districts marked by such circles, perimeters around loss.

America is one long quarrel, and those who leave do so as through a door slammed by an angry lover, meaning to return. But there are those too with no stake in the fight.

The long low-slung cruisers mean to arouse, along the

avenues, at the expense of future history, at any expense, a sentimental contempt.

To ease back into such captivity.

And to leave again?

Yes, but not tonight. Not so soon, if the leaving, too, is to be a form of bowing down.

THE LONG WAY ROUND

Tonight, as often now, he takes me aside and begins to explain the details of some bodily mechanism — this time it's lipids in the blood — using the true language of that craft, covering ground we've no doubt crossed before, but skipping nothing, defining again each unfamiliar term. He remembers before I do which parts I should already know but misremember. Travelling at high speed as though through a difficult interchange and taking the wrong turnoff: that's how information is mislaid. Often, too, I've become perfectly lost in cities I've lived in for years.

A sense of direction. Stories of his driving with a passenger, deep in accompanied monologue, then abruptly stopping when the conversation ends. Having already passed the destination by up to fifty miles. There is a direction to this talk, starting at a given point and then slowly making its way round the unsuspecting listener until, within sight of the origin, the circle may be completed in a single leap. This, I am told, is the same danger big game hunters face in the wild: the tiger's wide circle through the jungle.

The topic of lipids in the blood moves on to famine, the cultural mores which, in some circumstances, preclude survival. Which foods people will eat and which ones they will not touch though it would save them. And so on.

When his children were too young to be talked to in this way, he used to sing to quiet us, which only made us cry the louder. His favourite songs: "The hipbone's connected to the — kneebone..." and "It's a Long Way to Tipperary."

There is a book he has been searching for for several years. It contains biographical sketches of men and women who performed heroically in their professions, from light-house-keeper in the wilds to Newton seeing the moon fall like an apple toward the earth's center. He read it at the age of seven and it caused him to take the direction he did in life. *Benefactors of the World* is no longer listed in catalogues and is unknown to experienced bookfinders in several major cities. It is possibly a pirated edition. Since early childhood he has possessed a photographic memory, but even for him seventy years is a long time to remember. If he could recall every word now he'd have no need of the book. I myself have found that the memory falters most crucially when everything depends on it, and that when you can't locate the book you need you must find the way to bring it into being.

MOSTLY IT IS THE FUTURE WHICH HAUNTS THIS HOUSE

On the hill the great house cannot sleep. Into the huge aban-doned living room, stray headlights stream like malformed pearls, jettisoned. Upstairs the windows, clear of the uncon-scious breath of sleepers, yield nothing. And the house's heart sinks, the heater igniting its echo in each room, for all it continues to protect with its mechanical warmth.

Through the basement frosty with dust, through the tin-selled cracks in glass, outside the garden has grown wild and rangy. The beast returning to its loneliness when beauty forsakes it.

Mostly what weeps are the raw bright fruits of the city night. Blue haze among the basement tools, smoke of half a century that does not disperse but clings among the silent stands of drill-bits, the Waltzing Matilda lathe. Among the foundations of childhood, where the units of measure are calculated, behind the face behind the cigarette between my father's lips.

AFTER DARK THE FLOWERS

After dark the flowers let their other scent into the air, as if thinking aloud. Wild roses, magenta and white, the white ones their furred ghosts. And the wheedling music of the insects, planning a city that was never meant to come to fruition in daylight. What dreamers they are. And yet, just listening to them, that glittering bank of lights comes back: whatever city you imagined first, in childhood, as the way in or out.

We went, didn't we, each of us, after something. Like a dog running after a stick which was nothing more than the faked motion of his master's throwing arm. We lost what we couldn't remember. We lost our intentions.

The stars approach, but only so near they don't ground themselves on the shallows. They let their cargo be unloaded from them. And what cargo they carried, back in those days! The hotel, white as an iced cake among the palms. The palms, their bark that fell away like netting, the fronds we'd find like huge whips on the ground after a storm.

All night the pines grow electric with insect noise: enough power for a whole city. But the barest beginning of dawn shuts them down, so the insects wait in silence and limbo beneath the bark as another personality takes over the earth. One with a baby blue sky and the pines twisted against it in the shapes of our old, powerful, outmoded longings.

LUST

Certain dreams presage true events.
If a woman, for instance, in mid-life
dreams that from her own body,
attached and tingling, a penis buoys up
with such lust as has followed her all her days,
like a naughty, dangerous puppy,
always at the heels,
and should she dream then from the other side,
not of Lethe between life and death
but of another, unnamed river, then upon waking
her allegiances may be realigned
as utterly as the magnetic poles of the earth.

And should it, the next night, occur
that her lover, overtaken by lust as seldom before, require,
because the small-walled house is bright with invited strangers,
that they step out for a moment where the blackened woods
are tethered all around in the eye of the storm
which has not yet finished with them,
and that her garments be taken down under this new government
too about to fall, of stars unevenly revealed in the shaky coup,
then the Seven Sisters, the Pleiades, of whom there are truly eight
but the eighth is clairvoyant and sickly,
then the Seven Sisters look down upon this scene and are jealous.

And the third thing,
this light in the brain which is like the eighth Sister,
a shimmer, an urge, not to be lost but found, so strong
that the lazily unwilling fingers comply to write this down,
this third thing is like the eighth Sister,
or the persistently dimming flashlight which ceased
— and would always cease —
to shed sufficient light on what they were
doing on their way to the woods.

INTERMITTENT RAIN

Rain hitting the shovel
leaned against the house,
rain eating the edges
of the metal in tiny bites,
bloating the handle,
cracking it.
The rain quits and starts again.

There are people who go into that room in the house
where the piano is and close the door.
They play to get at that thing
on the tip of the tongue,
the thing they think of first and never say.
They would leave it out in the rain if they could.

The heart is a shovel leaning against a house somewhere
among the other forgotten tools.
The heart, it's always digging up old ground,
always wanting to give things a decent burial.

But so much stays fugitive,
inside,
where it can't be reached.

The piano is a way of practising
speech when you have no mouth.
When the heart is a shovel that would bury itself.
Still we can go up casually to a piano
and sit down and start playing
the way the rain felt in someone else's bones
a hundred years ago,
before we were born,
before we were even one cell,
when the world was clean,
when there were no hearts or people,
the way it sounded

a billion years ago, pattering
into unknown ground. Rain

hitting the shovel leaned against the house,
eating the edges of the metal.
It quits,
        and starts again.

CHITONS

We found one, one summer,
my aunt and sister and I,
beachcombing for tiny minarets
and sea-ground glass
off Havensneck, dead.

Breathless, empty-headed, still squinting
from continuous wind, as after a long ride
one feels still in motion —
we dumped a mosaic onto the table.
The chiton like a bloated boot sole
washed up from somebody drowned.
Curious, unsure,

we took a kitchen knife
and sliced through
to the sudden organs:
orange and magenta.
With such colours, my sister said,
they had to be for sex,
and whooped once with delight.

Says Webster, *the related but more advanced*
cephalopod
has a depressed body, and the power to eject
a black, ink-like fluid to darken the water
and conceal itself when in danger.

58

Gumboots, the locals call them,
as opposed to *chiton*,
which leads us back to the ancient Greeks,
who wore a tunic or undergarment of the same name —

so we think of Sappho,
especially in winter, when the tide
and the old year are receding.
Then they can be found along the foam line,
where storms bury and unbury them,
big as a baby's foot
or the workboot of a large man —
or at nightfall,
above the tideline,
where they resemble footprints going out to sea,
and fill us with unease.

SNOWLIGHT ON THE NORTHWOOD PATH

Last night on our way to the bathroom after making love
the neighbour's house lights must have stolen
a little way through the kitchen window; as we passed,

the two white bentwood chairs I had brought
with me from Vermont and another life
glowed with a faint, ulterior, mineral half-life —

illusion of a snowed-in night without moon in Vermont.
As once, after a convivial late night with friends,
my companion and I stepped out to a world

not as we'd left it; for while we drank and talked,
obliviously, snow had been falling,
and it had grown clear again, and very cold,

so that the ground glowed, risen several inches.
We weren't dressed for it,
yet chose to walk back by way of the woods,

whose paths, muddled of late by too much use,
had been obliterated by snow, so that we sank
deeper at each step, laughing.

Last night on our way back through the kitchen,
after the brightness of the bathroom, our eyes would not
    adjust;
the chairs had melded with the dark, and we stumbled.

Yet back in bed as I turned toward sleep
the paths became confused again,
my former life drifting across our life:

I was young, half-dreaming,
and because I had no past to speak of I went forward,
into a cold so extreme

it was at the same time exotically warm —
as though there were no way to distinguish
between the pleasure and the ache,

or to choose, last night,
in the after-ache of pleasure,
between my life and my life.

WE'RE OUT WITH THE NIGHT BEINGS

We're out with the night beings,
pale airborne zig-zags,
the staggered race through headlights,
once or twice a coyote,
the colour of straw, as ragged,
beings that cross us always from left to right,
barely missed by windshield or tires,
identified by stripe or snout or size
or not at all.
It was in Truth Or Consequences, New Mexico
we tried to stop,
after a rained-out rodeo, local festivities.
Finally found a room, though there was trouble
with a missing key. Unlocked the door to a boy
sitting up suddenly drunk in the dark
on a bed we had bought for the night.
He's not the kind to hurt you, said the desk clerk,
who was also a mother and mistress to a small silent dog
in a rhinestone collar, from behind a display
of earrings on a dead cholla branch,
and anyway he's gone.
We were tired, but took our money and moved on,
because we could,
not sentenced to that town,
we thought, as the boy was, probably for life.
We moved on
with the night beings from the other world,
which is also our world,
with speed and inattention,
one of those beautiful emptying hand puppets
now and then by the roadside,
"Guernica," as Klee might have painted it, for a windshield,
through desert where motels grow
arid and square with names like The Sands and Oasis.

MOON

Rising unperturbed from the
rubble of the construction site,
you take us by surprise,
above the blocky angles of a city hospital,
over swamps, villages in foreign countries
where we've felt foreign,
unable even to ask for an apple or a toilet,
or at the head of Vulcan Stairway
in the San Francisco night
made wise by you,
and the knowing flowers
which stand like death masks.
In the least probable places you appear,
simultaneous,
everywhere at home,
everywhere equal.
Bright nude, round and full as a Reubens,
I've seen you recline even as you were borne up.
You demonstrate the false science of levitation.
Or, inert, a wan
sliver, aloft in pale blue, lost in our days,
while we think only of our own effort,
our clocks, our meals...
That you move
not by degree, as we do,
not in steps, or by leaping,
but in one long frictionless
departure, a constancy
as irksome as a tapping foot,
and this alien calm
would drive us mad —
What of other moons?
Do they fall as you fall,
like the white petals
of the spring apricot,
like a discus,

or the end of romantic love
as seen from tedious, lifeless planets?
Why is it that you look so far away
when only hours ago you
burst into our rooms and silences —
and we felt our humanity,
the conspiracy of our being.

SAVE US FROM

Save us from night,
from bleak open highways
without end, and the fluorescent
oases of gas stations,
from the gunning of immortal
engines past midnight,
when time has no meaning,
from all-night cafes,
their ghoulish slices of pie,
and the orange ruffle on the
apron of the waitress,
the matching plastic chairs,
from orange and brown and
all unearthly colours,
banish them back to the test tube,
save us from them,
from those bathrooms with a
moonscape of skin in the mirror,
from fatigue, its merciless brightness,
when each cell of the body stands on end,
and the sensation of teeth,
and the mind's eternal sentry,
and the unmapped city
with its cold bed.
Save us from insomnia,
its treadmill,
its school bells and factory bells,

from living rooms like the tomb,
their plaid chesterfields
and galaxies of dust,
from chairs without arms,
from any matched set of furniture,
from floor-length drapes which
close out the world,
from padded bras and rented suits,
from any object in which horror is concealed.
Save us from waking after nightmares,
save us from nightmares,
from other worlds,
from the mute, immobile contours
of dressers and shoes,
from another measureless day, save us.

AUTUMN INCIDENTS

I went walking through one of the winding,
wealthier districts. High up,
inside one of the houses: someone practising scales.
A fading, ordered loneliness as the houses gave way
to woods, the sidewalk became a path, and farther on,
a hunched shape, unmoving, as in grief or worse,
resolved in silence as I neared
into two — taken up entirely — and a pair of glasses,
lain aside no doubt for intimacy,
through which, as I stepped around them,
the forest floor appeared, magnified.
Where I'd seen that shape before I couldn't say,
a late-night thriller maybe, the single figure
hunched over the transmitter, tapping, again and again,
the fingers on the keys. This is what came back to me,
how clear it was, the signature of touch,
the need to be believed. I made my way then, down

and down toward the warmth of stalled traffic,
the lowland of the city. Day had lapsed almost into dusk.
Whole streets were lighting up suddenly below me.

THE LIMITS OF KNOWLEDGE, TILTON SCHOOL,
NEW HAMPSHIRE

At certain points in the universe longing condenses,
the shade sucked against the screen,
the plain dishevelled ruffles that frame
the window — because a girl sleeps here during the year,
a school, a desk, the simple chair whose
duty and forgiveness are the weight of all matter.
A month from now someone's daughter
will enter this room,
her hair will fall along her back,
she will sit in struggle with
thoughts not her own, the books in front of her,
hour after hour — medieval really,
this illimitable patience, as at the bedside
of the dying, whom one loves —
and how the skin and breasts are lit by faint
sensations, that which asks as well
for knowledge *through* another.
What can be discovered within four walls?
Walls a pale green found nowhere in
nature but in the wings of a rare
moth that startled me once,
near, as big as my hand,
and whose colouration
mimics it.
Let us call it
learning, redisposing oneself, hour after hour,
to be as one is urged, cajoled,
told. I have lived in this room,

made love here, the man sleeps beside me.
Will she sense our trespass as an opening?
Or will she, like the local girl who served our dinner,
a few dollars and a summer job with which to
dabble in freedom,
think this town ugly,
because that is how she sees her life so far,
and she has not lived elsewhere.

AUTUMN

One night goes on longer than the rest, never so long,
whiled away. Then dawn.
Goodbye, insects. Hollow casings on the windowsill,
a dainty leg among the spice jars.
Goodbye, marigolds, the earth will not wait for you.
Trains hurtle by at the edges of cities,
the taste of bourbon, a mouthful of leaves.
Above everyone's dining table a chandelier burns.
Now the luxurious old wine can be uncorked,
the slicing of meat and bread, uncorked,
and in the black panes life goes on.

POEM BEGINNING WITH A LINE BY
ANNE MICHAELS

I cry for my father because of everyone's short sleeves.
Because of legs and the solemn, thoughtless act of walking.
Because shops are full of goods and they keep ordering
    more.
Because there is a new kind of metal,
and ties still hang in closets,
and it is Tuesday.
Because of the existence of books,
of boxer shorts, and fedoras, and baseball season,

which will begin again.
Because "dust" is a euphemism
and "cremains" is a new noun
that wasn't in the old dictionary,
because they fit into a gold box the size of a Steuben sculpture.
Because "ashes" is a euphemism
and the box is unexpectedly heavy
and California is flooded
and the fragments are in the rain.
Because bone is variously tubular and spongy
and glows in the dark.
Because it is edible and can be read by.
Because it is possible to throw away someone's false teeth
but not their glasses.

AFTER A DEATH

Seeing that there's no other way,
I turn his absence into a chair.
I can sit in it,
gaze out through the window.
I can do what I do best
and then go out into the world.
And I can return then with my useless love,
to rest,
because the chair is there.

HOUSE

Thinking of the wild grasses of
my childhood hillside,
my father's ashes
mingling with the soil,
I come again upon
the child I was, asleep

between impermeable walls,
who wakens, paralyzed with
terror in the summer night:
two inches of incarnate dread
against the whiteness of the sheet,
that rigid small voice
calling for my father.
Wordless they come to us,
the moth adhering to the mirror's surface,
an albino spider caught in the long
straws of a broom:
cool as grass.
I lie awake and listen
to my own house shift and settle.
A complete world of faucets and switches,
stairways into warmth,
what we think of as safety.
Greetings,
I say,
to the invisible cracks,
the delicate mask-like being that will
pause, and enter.

PINE

Pine, asleep in the sunshine,
I think I'll lie down near you and sleep awhile.

I've been hardheaded of late, surprised by an empty heart.
Tired of everything I know.

AND

       up through the field once more.
Sat in impressions where deer have lain.
Broken windowpane. Sungazing.
The town of Gualala,
hidden beyond ripples of forest.
So,
goodbye to berry picking,
visions of plenitude from the station wagon window,
those singular, wild meals,
the time we stumbled on the site
of the long-burnt-down cabin,
someone that slept through death,
and oh those yellow plums sweetened on disaster,
the looks between us then,
goodbye to memory.
          And yet much
stays with us. That
August is for huckleberries,
where the best apples are, that delicate
complete skeletons are to be found in the winter rain.
The back left leg of the woodstove, though,
must be propped with stones,
the well water turns bourbon purple.
It hardly matters, you'd say,
indoors or out,
one never has to *dress* here.
The light of a reading lamp,
and I a wall away, under the meteor shower,
my flesh of your flesh,
each rare event plotted and erased.
To think *never again* or *friendless*,
to think *my mother's cool hands*,
and, like a secret, the earth orchids
year after year that come
up again under the redwoods,
but they won't find you.

INTENT, OR THE WEIGHT OF THE WORLD

The other week in a department store
I picked up a pair of shoes from a clearance table
and couldn't tell
whether they were ugly or beautiful.
Stricken by this
inability to *see*,
and all the hands groping around me,
I spent the rest of the day
wandering from store to store.

Nonetheless it was the first day I could see
a way out of winter —
buds silhouetted along branches overhead —
and I remarked to several people
how warm it was,
the first spring-like day of the year.
A woman who worked in a bookstore
said she'd had to *run* back from lunch
it had been so cold.
Still, the clouds wore a soft blossoming look.
Later, a freezing wind.

On friends' recommendations
I'd been going from book to book,
movie to movie,
different prescriptions
but no cure.

It had been like gradually
losing the use of an arm,
like a piece of equipment that isn't working,
when everything looks okay on the outside,
so the problem must be farther in.
Someone I knew
who'd been depressed for several years
told me the story of how

one day he was playing tennis,
and all at once,
seemingly in one thwack of the ball,
back up through the arm,
sensation rushed into him.

All around me people passed
with tightened lips, concentrating hard.
The two parrots that lived upstairs
conversed in unrelated syllables,
chains of abusive, deficient,
mutant English —

Went to the zoo,
and while my friends were watching the gorillas
I couldn't take my eyes from the kids,
snorting, scratching their armpits,
aping cartoons.

I wanted to
hold my mind up next to other minds;

I remembered all the unfinished projects
grudgingly;

things that passed between people,
a look,
a breeze of understanding,

like exotic delicacies
from paradise —

❖ ❖ ❖

It had been like boarding a jetliner
for a destination far from waking life.

At first my dreams were lush, tinged sometimes

with a morbid eroticism,
morally timid —

In the morning I would pluck
clinging hairs from the pillow;
for hours the afterglow of dreaming would accompany me.
In my encounters
I could have been a mere silhouette, backlit
by this radiance
that gradually decayed...

Trying to settle down with a book,
after a few sentences I'd feel put out;
I'd pick things up, a letter, a bookmark,
and simply let them drop...

Still, all things considered,
I felt "fine,"
just as when you answer the telephone
and, instead of the dreaded, anticipated voice,
it's a friend, whom you like — relieved,
you do suddenly feel "fine" —

Conversation was like that,
trying to pass someone coming toward you down an aisle,
who's trying to pass someone coming toward them down
    an aisle —

More and more I wanted to sleep,
but there were too many items on the agenda,
jumbled, troubling vectors of thought —

And then I did not dream at all.

Eventually I must have been captured, carried off
by sleep
but without dreams, sensations, or consent.
Sleep like a kind of vegetable amnesia.

And though it *happened* to me,
I could not *experience* it.

❖ ❖ ❖

I was reminded of an old friend
whose comment on the last few years was
"I'd go to the movies
and out of all the people in the theatre
I was the only one laughing."

Meanwhile everything worked normally,
supermarkets remained open,
electricity surged on command...

At an outdoor wedding
I desperately needed to
sneak a laugh.
I didn't dare
turn toward my companion;
glancing sideways I could tell
he too was avoiding contact,
the moment when we would
disgrace ourselves with laughter,
and the other guests
all standing entranced on the lawn...

I was so far inside myself.
Hours would pass, waiting to be lifted out of it;
I'd go to the window and back again,
or stumble over the cat.
I was *sorry* about everything.

Someone would ask for a match
and without thinking I'd give them a lecture.

Squirrels, in the live
foreign world, raced through the trees.

Whenever I forced myself to dress up
I could see that I was "pretty."
"Pretty," but stiff.
And if, by accident,
my thighs brushed together,
I was repulsed —

✦ ✦ ✦

More and more what stood out
were not people's looks or gestures
but what propped them up,

the grandiose belief in a saviour,

the assumption,
dumb, unyielding, vapid,
that everything is *caused*...

A man and a woman on a sidewalk, for example,
who've been introduced once or twice
and haven't quite sorted out each other's names:
even if they've met by chance,
immediately,
as though it had been planned,
their conversation angles
toward camouflaged probing;
bluffing a little, to show control
but also interest —

There must have been inklings, glimpses —

I could tell I was intentionally
overlooking evidence.

And then, one evening,
in a restaurant with live opera,
the performers were able to hold their smiles

even through strenuous arias.
Between acts I went up to compliment the singers,
who only glanced back distractedly, barely polite —
for an instant the discrepancy might have hurt me,
but afterwards I felt proud of myself,
and of them.
Their earlier look of delight
had been so moving:
such delight *existed*.

It was afternoon already,
after the hard rains.
We were watching the sun go down,
clouds outlined in red neon,
as my friend began abruptly, open-endedly, to laugh.
Laughter like a revolving door,
glee, irony, forgiveness —

And though I had not expected it,
had not willed it,
here and there along the branches,
pink blossoms had broken out

FALSE SPRING

One day a year,
unmarked on any calendar,
not necessarily the same
from valley to valley
or year to year,
it comes. Wafting.
A little warmth to the joints,
and sweaters and jackets wrap their arms
around the waists of pedestrians,
trees lean wistfully over paths,
and sunlight — sunlight everywhere,
like transubstantiated butter.
In college towns fraternities advertise
Spring Bash!
Free Beer For Co-eds!
Passengers lean from speeding windows,
the postman makes his rounds earlier than usual,
peanut butter and jelly sandwiches
taste good again, for a day,
the dead stay dead,
and in the branches, Spring —
: mute tremolo of fingers
: dashes hats off heads
: goes around lifting skirts
: ferries the clouds.

TIME ALONE

He goes travelling on business and, all at once, reaching into a cupboard or stooping for a crumb, I notice myself. Still, there are simple tasks: sew on the missing buttons, find a movie on TV —anything! well, almost anything — eat. Seemingly insurmountable blocks of time can be whittled away like this, piecemeal, with nothing but a small finger-nail file. Like Miyoshi, then, one buys a red apple, a present to oneself; tries on all the rarely worn but beautiful clothes; fashions complicated hairdos held in place only by the fingers. Imagine the blonde curls and tight linen suits! And his return, then. What, to him, is fixed, what he loves, from a distance — how frangible it is, the thighs and cuticles, the mysteries of the hairline. To study one's body, then, in great detail, memorizing it. And one can always shout out — with little hope, it's true, of being heard — *Farewell! Farewell!* to the small unruly clouds in their solemn pilgrimage.

CITY LIGHTS

To board the train for Toronto and glance over at the other
track as that train starts rolling and the woman there,
opposite, dozing, opens her eyes.
To look into eyes and know there are many directions.
To have it all at once: cinnamon buns
from the Harbord Bakery and the late poems of Wang Wei.
To step out, bringing traffic to a halt.
To bemoan with total strangers the state of the lettuce,
to be queried concerning the uses of star fruit,
and expostulate thereon.
To guide an unsteady gentleman across the street
and refuse payment in eternity.
To happen on the long light down certain streets as the sun is
      setting,
to pass by all that tempts others without a thought.
For cigar smoke and Sony Walkmans and random belligerence,
the overall sense of delighted industry
which is composed of idle hatred, inane self-interest,
compassion, and helplessness, when looked at closely.
To wait in queues, anonymous as the price code in a supermarket.
To board a bus where everyone is talking at once,
and count eight distinct languages, and not know any.
For the Chinese proprietress of the Bagel Paradise Restaurant,
who is known to her customers as the joyful
otter is known to the clear salt water of Monterey Bay.
To know that everyone who isn't reading, daydreaming,
or on a first date is either full of plans or
playing Sherlock Holmes on the subway.
For eerie cloudlit nights, and skyscrapers,
and raccoons, jolly as bees.
For the joy of walking out the front door and becoming
instantly, and resolutely, lost.
To fall, when one is falling,
into a safety net, and find one's friends.
To be one among many.
To be many.

MORNING GLORIES

Between night and morning the freshened airy streets lie quiet. All night the spasms of rain and thunder and the calm that follows. What is it summer will finally give birth to? At this hour I walk invisibly, protected and alone, following a faint scent of angel that precedes me through the streets. And here before your darkened house: one starry light left on to say you will return this time, that you are only far away in a city I have not seen.

Before dawn I climb to your back porch where the morning glories dangle dripping wires, like downed phone lines, in the exaggerated quiet after storm. The flowers are sleeping, bright and twisted, hooked through the matted vine, each a day of summer still to come. Yesterday's are puckered, tobacco-coloured, as if life passed through them too quickly, barely rippling the surface.

Wherever you are now, I see you walking out of sleep as from a city whose ruin I have not yet witnessed, to catch me stealing time with your morning glories. They are like blue summer thunder and hang there, taunting us for having limits.

TWO HORSES

The leaves band together and go eddying, skirting the ground, an inch above it, riding invisible paths and invisible Ferris wheels, they go scuffling down roads, whirling into fields. Across the hillsides the new bales, evenly spaced, give off a bodily heat. Leather fields of turned clay, like acres of hooves. Those two horses we see sometimes, running in the fields, those two who pressed their faces like long solemn loaves against the trailer window in the middle of the night — they frightened us half to death! With their firm bewildered freeness, they knew how to explore: they shamed us by merely looking in. How stiff we lay in our bed, clutching each other. While they, escaped and free, went trotting together along roads laid out by their strange benefactors, we who spare the apple trees their lives in the fenced fields, the last apples like painted wood with soft, striated brushstrokes. Those two horses pass us by with the scenery; they have each other.

Overnight everything has whitened in the web of first frost and suddenly the first travelling flakes are dizzying the air. The oil heater shudders on and off, making little dungeon-sounds, and down the length of the trailer the fridge hisses and trembles, propelling itself through time. Those horses appear again in the yard, their dirty cotton manes torn by burrs and seeds. Pawing the ground as if they didn't remember ... having simply lost whatever wild earth smell they were following. They sniff the last of our garden, the toothless cobs on their dried stalks. One of them, taking the lead, swivels his beautiful body, but they do not look back at us. We who built the orchards and the roads.

RUBBER BOOTS

In Ontario, in autumn,
black and limp, with shining curves,
they are the only footwear for the fields.

All year they have lain in
fishy heaps at the back of closets
and now halls and entryways
are lined with them, pair by pair,
dripping onto newspaper,
upright, leaning drunkenly together, or toppled,
helpless as dull black beetles,
their legs in the air.
I remember the morning
Jane fell in love, in San Francisco,
with a pair,
glazed, brilliant as lemons
in the shop window.
But what shines in a wild Pacific storm
would leak within minutes
when the world turns to mud
and sucks at the heels
in Elora or Owen Sound.
A gash is an unhappy thing,
especially in black rubber,
when boots are cheap:
the kind thing is to carve
the toes like jack-o'-lanterns
and let them leer
unexpectedly in hallways.
Nothing mourns like a boot
for its lost mate.
You must fill it with water,
and flowers.
Unlike other shoes,
they never smell of possession.
They have mapped the sodden marsh,
trod on ice.
You step into them,
sound and seamless,
with a double pair of thick socks.
You enter the Ark.

THE THINKER, STONE ORCHARD

Sunflowers' thick stems twisted over, wild yellow curls around the heavy heads, and paired leaves hunched behind like the shoulderblades of "The Thinker," those poised scales that weigh one thing against another, weigh bronze against air and find them equal, though never balancing. The sunflowers stoop toward summer's end. Nearby, sunrays burn in and out of the copper eyes of a frog, hanging stiff as a little drowned man in the water. Kim, as on all other afternoons, bent over a problem, something with equations, which he spreads across the page, looking between them for the lost error. His shoulders still balancing one thing against another. He loves me. Life will not last.

On the far side of the house two cats roll in sunshine in the catnip patch — they would roll there forever if catnip didn't work its hazy forgetful pleasures — and then they stalk off, stiff-legged, drunkards. Not a yard away, in shadow, the weeds sprout their ragged hearts. The dark part of the garden, left to go to seed — smoky moth, spider in a gauzy net. The place everyone's eye passes over as it makes its rounds. The blind spot. Where everything we do not care to look at lives.

Nighttime, summer countryside. Insects sticking like magnets to the lit screens of the house. In the dark garden it's like standing at the weedy bottom of a well, staring straight up. Kim's shoulders with that athletic tension in them that never gives out. Not just some. All the stars.

After ten afternoons Kim has found the error and moved on, engrossed again. Boxcars of an almost endless train in the distance, metal grumbling about being next to metal. Beyond the mown fields, web of trees, down along the railbed the grey, glinty-eyed rocks, full of frozen forms. Faint moon, exactly torn in half.

CITY

Rushes of silver light. A little wind plays by itself in the corner of the plaza with whatever: lost leaves, bits of wrapper. Tall shocks of light from the buildings which are only mirrors trying to come clear. A gull, squawking, dips around the Royal Bank tower. Here and there the bombed-out look of bare structure, steel waiting for glass. Only the clues. A pair of trousers stuffed into a hedge, no explanation. A single shoe overturned on Yonge Street, passed back and forth all night by the wheels of opposing cars, now left alone in the morning light, pointing north.

North along the clean dirt road that led us one day to a meadow, unfindable again, dyed cherry-colour by the fallen sun, our shadows dark red, matching the blood inside. A few birds trickled from tree to tree, lost bits of a waterfall. Tunnelling worms that know nothing and see nothing, in those bare apples left to the branches. A queer country darkness came down around us. Hidden creatures turning up their volume, the fields on either side of the road competing in opposing keys. The lens of the earth's gases, before which we sat in the meadow, myopic, watching the stars flicker like movie screens in a far-off future. Given the chance you'd take a one-way trip there over the rest of your life on earth, you said. How beautiful, I thought, glancing over at Toronto. To inhabit that plane of lights intersecting nothing.

TRAVELLING

Past midnight I sink my head into the feather pillow. At last!
We are all solitary travellers. The motel lights have dimmed.
A key in another door: someone letting himself in, at any
hour. Just alongside my right ear, or beside the night table
with its standing glass of water, or just outside the sliding
glass door, loud and wide in the dark, the river, fed by
mountains, without beginning or end, knowing not its own
name, or lore, or the name of the town, or my name.

DAWN IN THE MASSIF CENTRAL

Hiked for three days
in the fierce warm wind.
Saw lightning,
black butterflies,
burning blue wildflowers,
cow chimes.
Saw a cave
where a prehistoric stream had carved
the initial outline,
a spotted horse,
saw the handprint.

Couldn't sleep
for what I had seen.

GROVE

It is a matter of spaces. Of infinitesimal nutrients built up
over time. Of constant sound, as of hinges or newborn
beings. How pleasant it is to be lost among the powerful
sunlit columns. Nothing is obscured except by grandeur,
nothing concealed. Pleasant, that is, unless you stray too
long and dusk begins, which fills the legs with sand. Yet if
you can stand just a little indiscriminate terror, if you can
endure not knowing (never to know) whether you are being
honoured on this earth or not so much as marked in pass-
ing: either way. And it will reveal itself, the alien, tribal
nature of the grove. Stars called into being above the sway-
ing crowns.

THE TREES

Their lives are longer, slower than ours.
They drink more deeply, slowly,
are warmed, do not shiver at dusk.
The heart unwinding makes a small noise.
Who would hear it?
Yet the trees attend,
perhaps to us, perhaps to nothing,
fragrance maybe, not of
flowering, but leaves and bark.
Trees. Dusk. Hand-coloured photographs
of the world before we were born.
Not sweet, but as water is,
sweet to a mouth long closed on itself.
Befriend them.

CLOSE TO THE BEGINNING

I'm standing on the muscled
rock sloping down to the water,

rock like the petrified
haunches of mammals,
marbled, sedimentary,

as if, in rugged prehistory
with its abstract cataclysms,
behemoths, mammoths
tumbled here to extinction.

The idea
that nothing actually leaves the earth
I misunderstood profoundly,
at an age when I had barely
grasped my own name,
following my mother over the rocks.

Taken literally,
it becomes a kind of myth,
uncorrected at its depths,
beckoning,

so that even now,
when I come upon such a cove,
in the escalating roar
and the transformed rocks,

I see her, large-boned, moving ahead of me.

FROM THE ISLAND

From here the city appears a chalky fortress, incandescent against thunder-bearing skies which admit, now and then, briefly, beams whose apparent purpose is to cauterize excessive beauty from the grass and then move on, though how one patch of grass differs from another is anyone's guess. This weather holds the subtle power of an egg, or seed, a hand stayed in anger, an inscrutable intent before which all rays and beams, all special effects, seem child's play, or else half bluff, like the courting gestures of the peacock or the newt ... the antics of my two grown male friends, for instance, who cavort across the grass — shouts of *Isadora Duncan! Isadora Duncan!* — stripped of shirts, manners, career, all loves but a clandestine love for being unwilled in the sudden larger universe. Against such skies the cottonwoods grow ponderous, the willows barely breathing. No more to bend in an attitude of solitude. No more to serve as objects of yearning! Like them we're free to be misled utterly, to continue on our chosen path, as if forever, without hindrance ... to stroll among the darkening office towers and condominiums across the water, where manners, career, shirts in the morning all unfold — and remark, of nothing in particular, like passersby before yet another of those perpetually unfinished public buildings, "Yes, but what's it for?" or "I'll bet that's costing the taxpayers a pretty penny!"

LEAVING THE ISLAND

And then approaches the last ferry, our antics die down, and we wait quietly, if a little reluctantly, but tired and ready, for we are not perpetual motion machines, as the ferry glides in for that random thud, wood against wood, the signal that we can board. Or we could board, except for the uniformed gentleman who, every twenty minutes, back and forth from the mainland, holds departing and prospective passengers at bay, with great ceremony, and finally, at his pleasure, unhooks the rope.

Engine, captain, lifebuoys aside, the essence of the ferry is wood, which floats upon water, and whose varnished grain, in the last rays, gives off such homesickness. Homesickness for the forest, for that primeval state which we have just shaken off so that we might return to the city, to a life in which each transaction must be earned and paid for.

The brief return trip is thus imbued with the momentousness of our voluntary parting from what we think of so fondly as our true nature; a willful sacrifice, an anguish indistinguishable from the ease of coming back to a familiar life. At sundown another ship drifts nearby. Music comes from it, and soon there will be dancing. The ship is tiered, lit up like the birthday cake of a prince or a queen as seen from childhood, a childhood in which only what was codified seemed beautiful. For back then we had to build everything up from nothing, ignorant of the means, that the goal might be merely to reach these very moments in which we flirt with the impulse to demolish all. That foolish notion of courage. And yet finally our image of happiness is complete, insatiable! To live it all again, but this time with full consciousness, *saturated* with consciousness.